EXPLORING TAPESTRY OF PEACE

GLOBAL PERSPECTIVES ON HARMONY

DR. MINAKSHI BANSAL

Made with ♥ on the Notion Press Platform
www.notionpress.com

DEDICATION

To all those who tirelessly strive for peace, who believe in the power of compassion, and who envision a world united in harmony.

ᐯᐯᐯ

Contents

Contents

Prayer

"Om Bhadram Karnebhih Shrinuyama Devah

Bhadram Pashyemakshabhiryajatrah

Sthirairangais Tushtuvamsastanubhih

Vyashema Devahitam Yadayuh

Svasti Na Indro Vriddhashravah

Svasti Nah Pusha Vishwavedah

Svasti Nastarkshyo Arishtanemih

Svasti No Brihaspatir Dadhatu

Om Shantih Shantih Shantih"

This mantra is a prayer for universal well-being, invoking the blessings of various deities for protection, health, and happiness. It emphasizes the importance of experiencing the auspicious through all senses and living a life aligned with divine purpose. The repetition of "Shantih" at the end signifies a deep desire for peace in the individual, the environment, and the universe at large. This mantra is often recited as a prayer for peace, prosperity, and the physical and spiritual well-being of all beings.

ᎠᎠᎠ

About The Author

Dr. Minakshi Bansal, born in the bustling metropolis of Delhi, India, has led a life steeped in artistry, scholarly pursuit, and an unwavering commitment to societal betterment. Following her marriage, she relocated to Ahmedabad, Gujarat, where she has since blossomed into a multifaceted beacon of inspiration for many. Dr. Minakshi is not only recognized as a gifted artist in the realm of Fine Arts but also as an esteemed author, a devoted social worker and a dedicated research scholar in Psychology. Her journey, marked by a profound dedication to elevating those around her, especially the downtrodden and underprivileged children of society, is a testament to her deep-seated belief in the transformative power of engagement and empathy.

From her earliest days, Minakshi was distinguished by an insatiable appetite for reading. Her literary universe was inhabited by characters and narratives that spanned ethical tales, motivational and inspirational stories, and the mythic parables imbued with life lessons. This voracious reading habit was not merely for personal edification but was driven by a desire to distill and disseminate the essence of these narratives to foster the development of students and peers alike. She was particularly captivated by the lives and teachings of historical figures and spiritual leaders such as Adi Shankaracharya, Swami Vivekananda, Dr. APJ Abdul Kalam, Mahamana Pandit Madan Mohan Malviya, Mahatma Gandhi, Sardar Vallabhai Patel, and Vinoba Bhave, among others. Their philosophies and life stories fueled her ambition to embody their ideals of resilience, selflessness, and relentless pursuit of knowledge.

Dr. Minakshi's academic and practical engagement with psychology has been equally noteworthy. As a research scholar, her focus has been on exploring the intricate tapestry of the human psyche, aiming to unlock the potential for psychological well-being and societal harmony. Her scholarly work is complemented by her active involvement in social work, where she employs her academic insights to make tangible differences in the lives of the underprivileged. Her endeavours in social work are characterized by an innovative approach that combines traditional wisdom with contemporary psychological practices to address the multifaceted challenges faced by these communities.

Her artistic talents, another facet of her diverse capabilities, are not merely a personal passion but also serve as a medium through which she communicates and connects with others. Her art, rich in symbolism and emotional depth, reflects her philosophical inquiries and social concerns, offering viewers a glimpse into the breadth of her intellect and the depth of her compassion.

In addition to her contributions to the arts and social sciences, Dr. Minakshi has embraced the healing arts of Pranic Healing, mastering the techniques developed by Master Choa Kok Sui. This practice, which focuses on the manipulation of Prana or life energy to heal the body and aura, has been both a personal journey of discovery and a means through which she extends her healing touch to others. Her proficiency in Pranic Healing is complemented by her advocacy and teaching of various forms of meditation aimed at rejuvenation, personal betterment, and the cultivation of harmony within individuals and communities alike.

Dr. Minakshi's life is a narrative of relentless pursuit, not just of personal achievement but of the upliftment and empowerment of society at large. Her diverse interests and talents—spanning the arts, literature, psychology, and the healing practices—converge on a singular path of service. She embodies the spirit of the luminaries who inspired her, channelling their legacy through her actions and teachings. Through her books, art, and social initiatives, she continues to inspire a new generation to embark on their own journeys of self-discovery, resilience, and altruism.

Her commitment to social betterment, particularly her focus on uplifting underprivileged children, reflects a deep understanding of the transformative potential of education and personal development. By integrating her knowledge of psychology, her artistic sensibilities, and her healing practices, Dr. Bansal has developed a holistic approach to social work that addresses both the immediate needs and the long-term well-being of the communities she serves.

As an author, Dr. Minakshi's writings offer a blend of inspirational insights, practical wisdom, and reflective contemplations drawn from her extensive reading and life experiences. Her books serve as a guide for those seeking to navigate the complexities of life with grace, resilience, and purpose. Through her narratives, she extends an invitation to her readers to explore the depths of their own potential and to contribute meaningfully to the collective well-being of society.

In Dr. Minakshi Bansal, we find a remarkable synthesis of the artist, the scholar, the healer, and the social activist. Her life's work stands as a beacon of hope and a source of inspiration for individuals seeking to make a difference in the world. Her story is a compelling reminder of the power of individual action, rooted in compassion and driven by a profound commitment to the betterment of humanity. Dr. Minakshi's legacy is not just in the tangible outcomes of her efforts but in the enduring spirit of inquiry, empathy, and service that she embodies.

ððð

Preface

In a world often marred by conflict and division, the pursuit of peace remains a universal yearning. It is a pursuit that transcends borders, cultures, and ideologies, uniting humanity in a shared aspiration for harmony and understanding. This book, born out of a deep-seated belief in the transformative power of peace, is an invitation to explore the multifaceted dimensions of this elusive yet essential concept.

My journey towards understanding peace has been a lifelong endeavor, shaped by personal experiences, encounters with diverse cultures, and a profound fascination with the human spirit's capacity for compassion and resilience. As a woman, I have witnessed firsthand the unique challenges and contributions that women bring to the pursuit of peace. I have seen how women, often marginalized and excluded from formal peace processes, have played pivotal roles in their communities as peacemakers, mediators, and healers.

This book is a culmination of my reflections and research on peace, drawing on insights from a wide range of disciplines, including history, philosophy, psychology, sociology, and spirituality. It is an attempt to weave together a tapestry of diverse perspectives on peace, highlighting the common threads that unite us in our shared aspiration for a more harmonious world.

The chapters that follow explore the various dimensions of peace, from the individual to the global. We delve into the ancient wisdom of diverse cultures, seeking timeless teachings on harmony that resonate across centuries. We examine the role of language in both inciting conflict and fostering peace, and explore how communication and conflict resolution can bridge divides and build understanding. We seek solace and inspiration in nature's symphony, recognizing the profound connection between a healthy environment and peaceful coexistence.

We journey inwards, exploring the cultivation of inner peace through mindfulness, gratitude, and compassion. We recognize the transformative power of forgiveness as a path to reconciliation and healing, both within ourselves and in our relationships with others. We celebrate the inspiring stories of changemakers who have dedicated their lives to peace, demonstrating the impact that individual and collective action can have on creating a more just and harmonious world.

We delve into the economics of peace, recognizing that prosperity flourishes in an environment of cooperation and stability. We examine the intricate relationship between peace and justice, acknowledging that a truly peaceful world must also be a fair and equitable one. We explore the vital role of women in peacebuilding, their unique leadership styles, and the power of feminine perspectives in creating lasting peace.

We learn from indigenous wisdom, drawing on ancient traditions that emphasize interconnectedness, community, and respect for nature. We explore the potential of technology to connect a global community, facilitating dialogue, amplifying voices for peace, and promoting understanding across cultures. We discover simple practices for incorporating peace into our everyday lives, through mindfulness, gratitude, forgiveness, and acts of kindness.

As we look towards the future, we acknowledge the emerging trends and challenges that will shape the path towards peace. Technological advancements, social movements, and global cooperation offer promising avenues for peacebuilding, but they are juxtaposed with persistent threats such as climate change, inequality, and political polarization. Navigating these complex challenges requires a multi-faceted approach that addresses the root causes of conflict, promotes inclusivity and diversity, and fosters a culture of peace.

This book is not a comprehensive guide to peace, nor is it a prescriptive manual for achieving it. Rather, it is an invitation to engage in a dialogue about peace, to explore its many dimensions, and to consider our own role in creating a more peaceful world. It is my hope that this book will inspire readers to reflect on their own understanding of peace, to embrace the diversity of perspectives presented, and to find their own unique ways of contributing to a more harmonious and equitable world.

Ultimately, peace is not a destination, but a journey. It is a continuous process of learning, growing, and evolving. It requires courage, compassion, and a willingness to challenge our own assumptions and biases. It is my sincere hope that this book will serve as a guide and inspiration for all those who seek to embark on this journey, weaving their own threads into the tapestry of peace.

Dr. Minakshi Bansal
Social Activist
Ahmedabad, Gujarat, Bharat

❧❧❧

ONE

Threads of Unity: Understanding Peace Across Cultures

Peace, a universal aspiration, takes on diverse forms across cultures. Yet, underlying these variations, there exist common threads that unite humanity in its pursuit of harmony. Exploring these shared values and practices can deepen our understanding of peace and foster greater cooperation between diverse societies.

At its core, peace is the absence of violence and conflict, but it also encompasses a state of well-being, both individually and collectively. This holistic concept is reflected in various cultural traditions. For instance, the concept of "Shalom" in Judaism goes beyond the mere absence of war, encompassing prosperity, health, and completeness.

Similarly, in many Indigenous cultures, peace is inextricably linked to a harmonious relationship with nature, recognizing the interconnectedness of all living beings.

One of the most fundamental threads of unity in understanding peace across cultures is the value placed on respect. Respect for oneself, for others, and for the environment is a cornerstone of peaceful coexistence. This includes respecting cultural differences, acknowledging diverse beliefs and practices, and valuing the contributions of all members of society. When respect is absent, conflict and violence often arise.

Another common thread is the importance of communication and dialogue. Open and honest communication allows for understanding, cooperation, and conflict resolution.

This can take many forms, from informal conversations to formal negotiations, but the underlying principle is the same: to foster understanding and build bridges between individuals and communities.

Forgiveness is another powerful tool for peacebuilding. The ability to forgive past wrongs and move forward is essential for reconciliation and healing. This does not mean forgetting or condoning harmful actions, but rather choosing to let go of resentment and anger, allowing for the possibility of a new beginning.

Many cultures emphasize the importance of inner peace as a prerequisite for outer peace. This involves cultivating qualities such as compassion, empathy, and mindfulness. Practices such as meditation, yoga, and prayer can help individuals develop inner peace, which can then radiate outwards to create a more peaceful society.

The role of education in promoting peace cannot be overstated. Education can equip individuals with the knowledge, skills, and values necessary to build peaceful communities. This includes teaching conflict resolution skills, promoting intercultural understanding, and fostering critical thinking and empathy.

Art and music have long been used as tools for peacebuilding. They can transcend cultural boundaries, evoke emotions, and inspire action. Music, in particular, has a unique ability to unite people, fostering a sense of shared humanity.

Spiritual and religious traditions often offer valuable insights into peace. While there are differences between faiths, many share common values such as compassion, forgiveness, and the pursuit of justice. Interfaith dialogue can help build bridges between communities and promote understanding and cooperation.

The pursuit of peace is not solely an individual endeavor; it also requires collective action. This includes working towards social justice, addressing economic inequality, and protecting the environment. When people feel that they are being treated fairly and that their basic needs are met, they are less likely to resort to violence.

The role of women in peacebuilding is increasingly recognized. Women often play a crucial role in conflict resolution and reconciliation, bringing unique perspectives and skills to the table.

Empowering women and ensuring their full participation in decision-making processes is essential for building sustainable peace.

Technology can be a powerful tool for peacebuilding. It can connect people across borders, facilitate dialogue, and raise awareness of global issues.

However, it can also be used to spread hate speech and misinformation. It is important to use technology responsibly and ethically in the pursuit of peace.

Ultimately, peace is a journey, not a destination. It requires ongoing effort and commitment from individuals, communities, and nations. By recognizing the common threads that unite us, we can work together to create a more peaceful and harmonious world.

ᗡᗡᗡ

Peace is not merely the absence of war, but a symphony of respect, communication, and forgiveness. It's a dance of diverse cultures united by the common thread of humanity. Let us weave together a tapestry of hope where every voice is heard and valued.

ᗡᗡᗡ

TWO

ANCIENT WISDOM: TIMELESS TEACHINGS ON HARMONY

Throughout history, ancient civilizations have grappled with the concept of harmony, weaving intricate philosophies and practices aimed at fostering peace and balance in both individual lives and society as a whole. These timeless teachings, passed down through generations, offer valuable insights into the nature of harmony and its essential role in human flourishing.

In ancient Greece, philosophers like Plato and Aristotle explored the concept of harmony as a fundamental principle of the universe. Plato's "Theory of Forms" posited that harmony was an ideal state of balance and proportion, reflected in both the natural world and human society. Aristotle's "Golden Mean" emphasized the importance of moderation and balance in all aspects of life, avoiding extremes and finding a harmonious middle ground.

In ancient China, Taoism and Confucianism offered

complementary perspectives on harmony. Taoism emphasized the importance of aligning oneself with the natural flow of the universe, embracing change and finding balance within oneself. Confucianism, on the other hand, focused on social harmony, emphasizing the importance of relationships, respect for authority, and adherence to social norms.

The ancient Indian philosophy of Hinduism also placed a strong emphasis on harmony. The concept of "Dharma" refers to one's duty or purpose in life, and fulfilling this Dharma is seen as essential for maintaining cosmic order and harmony. Hinduism also emphasizes the importance of non-violence (Ahimsa) and the interconnectedness of all living beings.

Buddhism, which originated in India, also teaches the importance of harmony. The Buddha's teachings emphasize the Four Noble Truths, which identify suffering as an inherent part of life and offer a path to overcome it through the Eightfold Path. This path includes practices such as right speech, right action, and right livelihood, all of which are aimed at cultivating inner peace and harmony.

Ancient Egyptian civilization also held harmony in high regard. The concept of "Ma'at" represented truth, justice, and cosmic order. Maintaining Ma'at was seen as essential for the well-being of both individuals and society as a whole. Ancient Egyptians believed that by living in accordance with Ma'at, they could achieve harmony with the divine and ensure the prosperity of their civilization.

Across these diverse cultures, there are common threads that run through their teachings on harmony. One is the recognition that harmony is not merely the absence of conflict, but a positive state of balance and well-being. This balance is not static, but dynamic, requiring constant adjustment and adaptation to changing circumstances.

Another common thread is the emphasis on interconnectedness. Ancient wisdom recognizes that individuals are not isolated entities, but part of a larger whole. This interconnectedness extends to family, community, nature, and the cosmos. Harmony is achieved when individuals recognize their place within this larger system and act in ways that contribute to the well-being of the whole.

Ancient teachings also emphasize the importance of inner peace as a foundation for outer peace. This involves cultivating qualities such as compassion, empathy, mindfulness, and self-awareness. Practices such as meditation, yoga, and prayer can help individuals develop inner peace, which can then radiate outwards to create a more harmonious society.

While these ancient teachings offer valuable insights, they are not simply relics of the past. They remain relevant in today's world, where conflict, violence, and environmental degradation threaten our collective well-being. By drawing on the wisdom of our ancestors, we can gain a deeper understanding of the nature of harmony and its essential role in creating a more peaceful and sustainable future.

The timeless teachings on harmony remind us that peace is not merely an abstract ideal, but a practical goal that can be achieved through individual and collective effort. By cultivating inner peace, fostering harmonious relationships, and working towards social justice and environmental sustainability, we can create a world where all beings can thrive.

ᎠᎠᎠ

Ancient wisdom whispers timeless truths about harmony, echoing through the ages. It teaches us to find balance within ourselves and in our relationships, to seek peace in nature's embrace, and to cultivate compassion for all living beings. Let us heed these ancient teachings and find our own path to inner peace.

❥❥❥

THREE

THE LANGUAGE OF PEACE: COMMUNICATION AND CONFLICT RESOLUTION

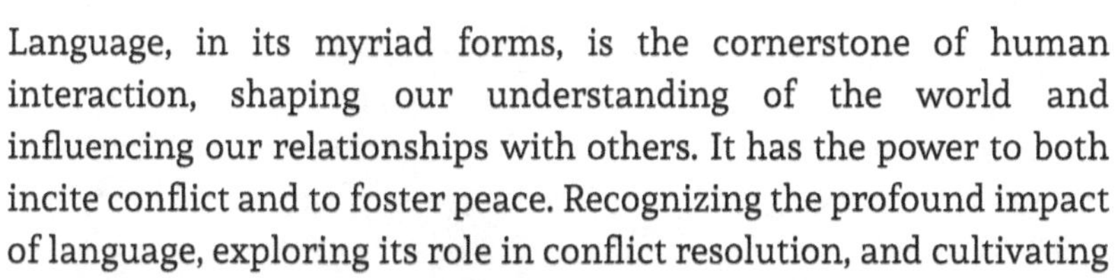

Language, in its myriad forms, is the cornerstone of human interaction, shaping our understanding of the world and influencing our relationships with others. It has the power to both incite conflict and to foster peace. Recognizing the profound impact of language, exploring its role in conflict resolution, and cultivating a language of peace are essential steps towards building a more harmonious world.

At its core, communication is the exchange of information, ideas, and emotions. Effective communication requires not only the ability to articulate one's thoughts clearly but also the capacity to listen attentively and empathetically. When communication breaks down, misunderstandings and conflicts can arise. This is particularly true in cross-cultural contexts, where differences in language, values, and communication styles can lead to misinterpretations and misunderstandings.

In the realm of conflict resolution, language plays a pivotal role. The way we choose to express ourselves can either escalate or de-escalate a conflict. Inflammatory language, personal attacks, and generalizations can fuel animosity and create further division. Conversely, using respectful language, acknowledging the other person's perspective, and focusing on the problem rather than the person can help to create an environment conducive to resolution.

Nonviolent communication (NVC), a communication model developed by Marshall Rosenberg, emphasizes the importance of expressing feelings and needs in a way that promotes understanding and connection. NVC encourages individuals to focus on their own feelings and needs, rather than blaming or judging others. This approach can be particularly helpful in resolving conflicts, as it allows for open and honest communication without escalating tensions.

Active listening is another crucial aspect of effective communication and conflict resolution. This involves not only hearing the words spoken but also paying attention to the underlying emotions and needs being expressed. Active listening requires suspending judgment, asking clarifying questions, and reflecting back what has been heard to ensure understanding.

Mediation and dialogue are two approaches to conflict resolution that rely heavily on language. Mediation involves a neutral third party who facilitates communication between the conflicting parties, helping them to identify their interests and needs, and to find mutually agreeable solutions. Dialogue, on the other hand, is a more open-ended process that allows for a deeper exploration of the issues at hand, fostering understanding and building relationships.

In addition to verbal communication, non-verbal communication also plays a significant role in conflict resolution. Body language, facial expressions, and tone of voice can convey emotions and attitudes that may not be expressed in words. Being aware of our own non-verbal cues and paying attention to those of others can help to improve communication and prevent misunderstandings.

Cultivating a language of peace involves not only choosing our words carefully but also fostering a mindset of respect, empathy, and understanding. This means avoiding language that dehumanizes or demonizes others, and instead focusing on shared values and common goals. It also means being willing to listen to different perspectives and to engage in constructive dialogue, even when there are disagreements.

The media plays a powerful role in shaping public discourse and influencing attitudes towards conflict. By choosing to highlight stories of reconciliation and cooperation, and by promoting respectful dialogue, the media can contribute to a culture of peace. Conversely, sensationalist reporting and inflammatory rhetoric can fuel animosity and exacerbate conflict.

Education also plays a crucial role in promoting a language of peace. Teaching children conflict resolution skills, intercultural communication, and media literacy can empower them to become peacebuilders in their own communities. By fostering a generation of young people who are skilled in communication and committed to peaceful solutions, we can create a more harmonious future for all.

The language of peace is not a utopian ideal, but a practical necessity in a world grappling with complex challenges. By recognizing the power of language, both to wound and to heal, we can consciously choose to use our words to build bridges of understanding, resolve conflicts peacefully, and create a more just and equitable world.

❧❧❧

Language has the power to both wound and heal. Let us choose our words carefully, crafting a language of peace that builds bridges of understanding and fosters reconciliation. In the symphony of human interaction, may our voices be instruments of harmony.

ÞÞÞ

FOUR

NATURE'S SYMPHONY: FINDING PEACE IN THE NATURAL WORLD

In the ceaseless hum of modern life, it's easy to forget the profound solace and tranquility offered by the natural world. Yet, throughout history, humans have found peace, inspiration, and even healing in nature's symphony. This intricate interplay of sights, sounds, and sensations provides a profound connection to something larger than ourselves, fostering a sense of peace that transcends the chaos of daily life.

From the gentle rustling of leaves to the rhythmic crashing of waves, nature's sounds have a calming effect on our minds and bodies. The Japanese practice of "shinrin-yoku," or forest bathing, highlights the therapeutic benefits of immersing oneself in the sights and sounds of nature. Studies have shown that spending time in nature can lower blood pressure, reduce stress hormones, and boost the immune system.

Beyond its physiological effects, nature also nourishes our souls. The awe-inspiring beauty of a mountain vista, the vibrant colors of a sunset, or the delicate intricacies of a flower can evoke a sense of wonder and appreciation for the world around us. This connection to something larger than ourselves can help us to put our own problems into perspective and find a sense of peace amidst life's challenges.

The natural world also offers a respite from the constant stimulation of modern life. In nature, we can disconnect from technology and reconnect with our senses. The simple act of walking barefoot on the earth, feeling the sun on our skin, or listening to the birdsong can be incredibly grounding and restorative.

Nature also provides a space for reflection and introspection. Away from the distractions of daily life, we can quiet our minds and connect with our inner selves. This can be a powerful tool for personal growth and self-discovery, helping us to gain clarity and find peace within.

Moreover, nature's rhythms and cycles offer a sense of order and predictability in a world that often feels chaotic. The changing seasons, the waxing and waning of the moon, and the ebb and flow of tides remind us that there is a natural order to things. This can be comforting and reassuring, helping us to find peace in the midst of uncertainty.

Spending time in nature can also foster a sense of interconnectedness. As we observe the intricate relationships between plants, animals, and the environment, we begin to see ourselves as part of a larger web of life. This realization can cultivate a sense of responsibility for the well-being of the planet and inspire us to take action to protect it.

Nature also offers a space for creative expression and inspiration. Many artists, writers, and musicians have found inspiration in the natural world. The beauty and complexity of nature can spark creativity and help us to see the world in new ways.

Moreover, nature can be a source of solace and healing in times of grief or loss. The natural world's resilience and ability to regenerate can offer hope and comfort in the face of adversity. The simple act of spending time in nature can help us to process our emotions and find a sense of peace amidst pain.

In a world that is increasingly urbanized and disconnected from nature, it is more important than ever to seek out opportunities to connect with the natural world. Whether it's a walk in the park, a hike in the mountains, or a weekend camping trip, spending time in nature can have a profound impact on our well-being.

The natural world offers a symphony of sights, sounds, and sensations that can soothe our souls, inspire our creativity, and connect us to something larger than ourselves. By immersing ourselves in nature's symphony, we can find peace, healing, and a renewed sense of wonder for the world around us.

ᐳᐳᐳ

Nature's symphony, a chorus of rustling leaves, crashing waves, and birdsong, offers solace and tranquility to weary souls. In the embrace of nature, we find peace, inspiration, and a deeper connection to the world around us. Let us protect this symphony, for it is our shared home.

FIVE

Inner Peace: Cultivating Harmony Within

In the relentless pursuit of external success and material possessions, the significance of inner peace often gets overshadowed. Yet, the quest for harmony within is as ancient as humanity itself. Inner peace, a state of tranquility and contentment that arises from within, is not merely an abstract concept but a tangible experience that can be cultivated through conscious effort and practice. It is a state of being where the mind is calm, emotions are balanced, and the spirit is at ease.

At its core, inner peace is about finding harmony within oneself. It involves understanding and accepting our thoughts, emotions, and experiences without judgment. It is about letting go of negativity, resentment, and fear, and embracing compassion, forgiveness, and gratitude. This journey of self-discovery and self-acceptance is not always easy, but it is essential for achieving lasting peace and happiness.

One of the fundamental steps towards cultivating inner peace is developing self-awareness. This involves paying attention to our thoughts, emotions, and physical sensations, and understanding how they influence our behavior and well-being. Mindfulness meditation, a practice that involves focusing on the present moment without judgment, is a powerful tool for developing self-awareness.

Another key aspect of inner peace is emotional regulation. This involves learning to manage our emotions in a healthy way, rather than letting them control us. Techniques such as deep breathing, progressive muscle relaxation, and cognitive reappraisal can help to reduce stress and anxiety, and promote emotional well-being.

Cultivating positive emotions such as gratitude, compassion, and joy is also essential for inner peace. Gratitude involves appreciating the good things in our lives, while compassion involves feeling empathy for others and wanting to alleviate their suffering. Joy is a deep sense of happiness and contentment that arises from within. By focusing on these positive emotions, we can counteract negativity and cultivate a more peaceful state of mind.

Letting go of negativity is another crucial step towards inner peace. This includes forgiving ourselves and others for past mistakes, releasing resentment and anger, and accepting what we cannot change. This does not mean condoning harmful behavior, but rather choosing to let go of the emotional baggage that weighs us down.

Developing a sense of purpose and meaning in life can also contribute to inner peace. This involves identifying our values, passions, and goals, and aligning our actions with them. When we feel that we are living a meaningful life, we are more likely to experience inner peace and contentment.

Spiritual practices can also play a significant role in cultivating inner peace. Prayer, meditation, and contemplation can help us to connect with something larger than ourselves and to find meaning and purpose in life. These practices can also help to reduce stress, anxiety, and depression, and to promote feelings of peace and well-being.

It is important to note that inner peace is not a static state, but a dynamic process. It requires ongoing effort and commitment to maintain. There will be times when we experience stress, anxiety, or other negative emotions. However, by developing the skills and practices mentioned above, we can learn to manage these emotions and return to a state of peace.

The benefits of inner peace are numerous and far-reaching. It can improve our physical health, reduce stress and anxiety, boost our immune system, and enhance our overall well-being. It can also improve our relationships, enhance our creativity, and increase our productivity. Moreover, inner peace can lead to a more compassionate and harmonious world.

In a world that is constantly bombarding us with information and demands, finding inner peace can seem like an elusive goal. However, it is a goal worth striving for. By cultivating inner peace, we can create a more fulfilling and joyful life for ourselves and for those around us.

ᗡᗡᗡ

Inner peace is not a luxury, but a necessity. It is the foundation upon which we build peaceful relationships, communities, and societies. Through mindfulness, gratitude, and compassion, we can cultivate a sense of harmony within ourselves that radiates outwards, touching the lives of all we encounter.

SIX

FORGIVENESS: THE PATH TO RECONCILIATION

Forgiveness, a concept woven into the fabric of human interaction, is a profound and transformative act that paves the way for reconciliation and healing. It is not merely about forgetting or condoning past wrongs, but rather a conscious decision to release resentment, anger, and the desire for revenge. Forgiveness is a journey that begins within oneself, extending outwards to mend broken relationships and foster a sense of peace and understanding.

At its core, forgiveness is an act of compassion, both towards oneself and towards others. It acknowledges that we are all fallible beings, capable of making mistakes and causing harm. By forgiving, we acknowledge our shared humanity and recognize that holding onto anger and resentment only perpetuates suffering.

Forgiveness is not a sign of weakness or surrender, but rather a demonstration of strength and courage. It takes immense inner strength to let go of the pain and hurt caused by another, and to choose a path of healing and reconciliation. Forgiveness does not mean forgetting or excusing the harm done, but rather choosing to release the negative emotions associated with it.

The path to forgiveness can be challenging and often requires time and patience. It involves acknowledging the pain and hurt caused by the offense, understanding the motivations behind the actions, and ultimately choosing to let go of the anger and resentment. This process can be facilitated by seeking support from others, engaging in self-reflection, and practicing empathy towards both oneself and the offender.

Forgiveness has profound benefits for both individuals and communities. On an individual level, forgiveness can lead to reduced stress, anxiety, and depression. It can also improve physical health, as holding onto anger and resentment has been linked to a variety of health problems. Furthermore, forgiveness can foster a sense of inner peace and well-being, allowing individuals to move forward from past traumas and build healthier relationships.

On a community level, forgiveness can play a crucial role in reconciliation and peacebuilding. In societies torn apart by conflict, forgiveness can break the cycle of violence and revenge, creating space for dialogue and understanding. By forgiving past wrongs, communities can begin to heal and rebuild trust, paving the way for a more peaceful and harmonious future.

Forgiveness is not a one-time event, but an ongoing process. It requires constant effort and commitment to maintain. There will be times when old wounds resurface and feelings of anger and resentment reappear. However, by cultivating a forgiving attitude and practicing compassion towards oneself and others, it is possible to overcome these challenges and continue on the path to reconciliation.

The importance of forgiveness is emphasized in many spiritual and religious traditions. In Christianity, forgiveness is a central tenet, with Jesus teaching his followers to forgive those who have wronged them. In Islam, forgiveness is considered a virtue, and Muslims are encouraged to forgive even their enemies. In Hinduism, forgiveness is seen as a way to purify the soul and achieve liberation.

Forgiveness is a universal human experience. Regardless of our cultural or religious background, we have all been hurt by others at some point in our lives. And we have all struggled with the question of whether or not to forgive. However, by understanding the transformative power of forgiveness, we can choose to release the past and embrace a future filled with peace, healing, and reconciliation.

ᛏᛏᛏ

Forgiveness is a gift we give ourselves and others. It liberates us from the chains of resentment and anger, allowing us to move forward with grace and compassion. Let us embrace forgiveness as a path to reconciliation and healing, for it is the cornerstone of peace.

SEVEN

THE ROLE OF ART AND MUSIC IN PEACEBUILDING

Art and music, often considered mere forms of entertainment or cultural expression, possess a profound and often underestimated power in the realm of peacebuilding. These creative mediums transcend linguistic and cultural barriers, evoke deep emotions, and foster connections that can heal wounds, bridge divides, and inspire collective action towards a more harmonious world.

Throughout history, art and music have been utilized as potent tools for social change and peacebuilding. From ancient cave paintings depicting scenes of communal harmony to modern protest songs calling for justice and equality, these creative expressions have served as a voice for the voiceless and a catalyst for change. They have the unique ability to capture the human experience in all its complexity, conveying both the pain and suffering caused by conflict and the resilience and hope that emerge from it.

Music, in particular, has a universal language that can touch hearts and minds across cultures. The rhythmic beats, melodic tunes, and evocative lyrics can evoke a wide range of emotions, from joy and celebration to sorrow and mourning. In times of conflict, music can provide solace and comfort, uniting people in shared grief and offering a sense of hope for a brighter future.

The power of music to heal and unite has been harnessed in various peacebuilding initiatives around the world. Music therapy, for instance, utilizes music to address a wide range of physical, emotional, and social needs. It has been used to help trauma survivors process their experiences, promote relaxation and stress reduction, and foster social connection and communication.

In conflict zones, music can be a powerful tool for reconciliation and dialogue. By bringing together individuals from different sides of a conflict to create music together, they can transcend their differences, find common ground, and build relationships based on mutual respect and understanding.

Art, in its various forms, also plays a crucial role in peacebuilding. Visual arts, such as painting, sculpture, and photography, can capture the human cost of conflict in a way that words alone cannot. They can evoke empathy and compassion, prompting viewers to question their own assumptions and biases, and to consider alternative perspectives.

Theater and performance art can also be powerful tools for peacebuilding. By creating a shared experience that explores themes of conflict, reconciliation, and hope, they can foster dialogue and understanding between different communities.

Public art installations, murals, and graffiti can transform public spaces into canvases for peace. By depicting images of hope, unity, and resilience, they can inspire communities to overcome adversity and work towards a more peaceful future.

Digital art and social media platforms have opened up new avenues for artistic expression and peacebuilding. Through online platforms, artists can share their work with a global audience, raising awareness of social issues and mobilizing support for peace initiatives.

The role of art and music in peacebuilding is not limited to professional artists and musicians. Community-based arts projects can empower individuals to express themselves creatively, build social connections, and contribute to the healing and transformation of their communities.

The power of art and music lies in their ability to touch our hearts and minds, to evoke emotions, and to inspire action. They offer a unique lens through which to view the world, challenging us to question our assumptions, to empathize with others, and to imagine a better future. By harnessing the transformative power of art and music, we can create a world where peace is not just a dream, but a lived reality.

ppp

Art and music, the universal languages of the soul, have the power to transcend boundaries and touch the depths of our humanity. They can evoke emotions, inspire action, and unite us in our shared quest for peace. Let us celebrate the transformative power of art and music in building a more harmonious world.

EIGHT

PEACE THROUGH EDUCATION: EMPOWERING FUTURE GENERATIONS

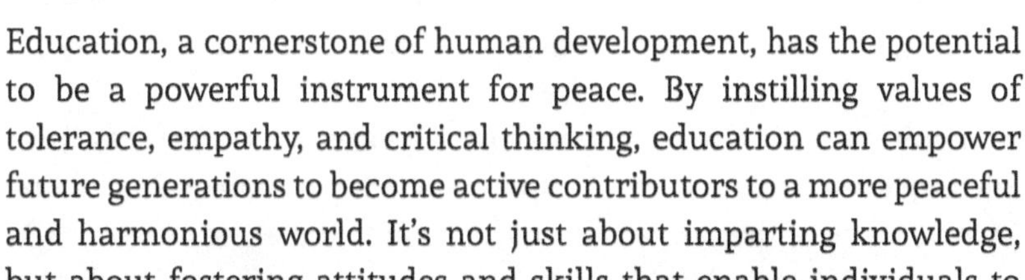

Education, a cornerstone of human development, has the potential to be a powerful instrument for peace. By instilling values of tolerance, empathy, and critical thinking, education can empower future generations to become active contributors to a more peaceful and harmonious world. It's not just about imparting knowledge, but about fostering attitudes and skills that enable individuals to understand, prevent, and resolve conflicts constructively.

At its core, peace education goes beyond traditional academic subjects. It focuses on developing a holistic understanding of peace, exploring its various dimensions – personal, social, political, and environmental. It encourages students to examine the root causes of conflict, such as inequality, injustice, and prejudice, and to explore nonviolent solutions.

One of the fundamental principles of peace education is fostering critical thinking and problem-solving skills. This involves encouraging students to question assumptions, analyze information from multiple perspectives, and evaluate the consequences of different courses of action. By developing these skills, students are better equipped to navigate complex issues and make informed decisions that contribute to peace.

Another key aspect of peace education is promoting empathy and understanding. This involves encouraging students to put themselves in the shoes of others, to understand their perspectives, and to appreciate their experiences. Empathy is a powerful antidote to prejudice and hatred, and it can foster a sense of connection and solidarity among diverse groups.

Peace education also focuses on developing communication and conflict resolution skills. This involves teaching students how to express their needs and concerns in a nonviolent way, how to listen actively and respectfully to others, and how to negotiate and compromise to find win-win solutions. These skills are essential for building healthy relationships and resolving conflicts peacefully.

In addition to these core principles, peace education can also encompass a wide range of topics, such as human rights, social justice, environmental sustainability, and global citizenship. By exploring these issues, students can develop a deeper understanding of the interconnectedness of all life and the importance of working together to create a more just and peaceful world.

Peace education is not just about theoretical concepts; it also involves practical action. Service learning, for instance, provides students with opportunities to apply their knowledge and skills to real-world problems, such as working with marginalized communities, advocating for social justice, or promoting environmental sustainability. These experiences can foster a sense of empowerment and agency, inspiring students to become active contributors to their communities and the world.

The role of teachers in peace education is critical. They serve as role models, mentors, and facilitators, guiding students on their journey towards peace. By creating a safe and inclusive learning environment, encouraging dialogue and debate, and modeling peaceful behavior, teachers can inspire students to embrace the values of peace and to become agents of change.

The impact of peace education extends far beyond the classroom. By empowering young people with the knowledge, skills, and values necessary to build peaceful communities, it can contribute to a more just and equitable society. Studies have shown that peace education can reduce violence and aggression, improve academic performance, and increase civic engagement among students.

Peace education is not a luxury but a necessity in today's world. As we face unprecedented challenges, such as climate change, social inequality, and political polarization, it is more important than ever to equip future generations with the tools they need to build a more peaceful and sustainable future.

Peace through education is a long-term investment in the well-being of humanity. By empowering young people to become peacebuilders, we can create a ripple effect that spreads throughout society, leading to a more harmonious and prosperous world for all.

ᗰᗰᗰ

Education is the key to empowering future generations to become architects of peace. By instilling values of empathy, critical thinking, and conflict resolution, we can equip our children with the tools they need to build a brighter future for all. Let us invest in peace education, for it is an investment in our collective well-being.

NINE

SPIRITUAL PERSPECTIVES ON PEACE: FINDING COMMON GROUND

Spiritual perspectives on peace offer a unique lens through which to understand and cultivate harmony, both within ourselves and in the world around us. While different spiritual traditions may vary in their specific beliefs and practices, they often converge on fundamental principles that emphasize the interconnectedness of all beings, the importance of compassion, and the pursuit of inner peace as a foundation for outer peace. Exploring these shared values can reveal common ground upon which individuals from diverse backgrounds can come together to build a more peaceful and harmonious world.

At the heart of many spiritual traditions lies the belief in the interconnectedness of all life. This interconnectedness extends beyond the human realm to encompass the natural world, the cosmos, and the divine. Recognizing this interconnectedness can foster a sense of responsibility for the well-being of others and the planet, leading to actions that promote peace and harmony.

Compassion, the ability to understand and share the feelings of others, is another core value emphasized in many spiritual traditions. It involves not only recognizing the suffering of others but also actively seeking to alleviate it. Compassion can be cultivated through practices such as meditation, prayer, and acts of kindness. When we approach others with compassion, we are less likely to engage in conflict and more likely to seek peaceful solutions.

Many spiritual traditions also emphasize the importance of inner peace as a prerequisite for outer peace. This involves cultivating qualities such as mindfulness, equanimity, and non-attachment. Practices such as meditation, yoga, and prayer can help individuals to quiet their minds, regulate their emotions, and develop a sense of inner calm. When we are at peace within ourselves, we are less likely to be reactive and aggressive, and more likely to respond to conflict with wisdom and compassion.

Forgiveness is another key theme in many spiritual traditions. The act of forgiving allows us to release resentment and anger, paving the way for healing and reconciliation. Forgiveness does not mean condoning harmful actions, but rather choosing to let go of the negative emotions associated with them. This can be a challenging process, but it is essential for building peaceful relationships and communities.

Spiritual traditions also offer insights into the nature of conflict and its resolution. They often emphasize the importance of understanding the root causes of conflict, such as greed, hatred, and ignorance. By addressing these underlying causes, we can create conditions that are more conducive to peace.

Many spiritual traditions also promote nonviolence as a way of life.

This involves not only refraining from physical violence but also avoiding harmful speech and thoughts. Nonviolence is not passive; it requires courage, discipline, and a commitment to finding peaceful solutions to conflict.

Interfaith dialogue and cooperation can also be powerful tools for peacebuilding. By engaging in respectful dialogue with people from different faith traditions, we can learn from each other, build bridges of understanding, and work together to address shared challenges.

Spiritual perspectives on peace can also inform our approach to social justice and environmental sustainability. Many spiritual traditions emphasize the importance of caring for the poor and vulnerable, protecting the environment, and promoting social equality. By aligning our actions with these values, we can contribute to a more just and peaceful world.

While spiritual perspectives on peace can offer valuable insights and guidance, it is important to acknowledge that religion has also been a source of conflict and violence throughout history. It is crucial to distinguish between the peaceful teachings of spiritual traditions and the actions of individuals or groups who may misuse religion to justify violence or discrimination.

The path to peace is a complex and multifaceted one. It requires individual transformation, social change, and political will. Spiritual perspectives on peace can offer a valuable framework for understanding and addressing the root causes of conflict, fostering compassion and forgiveness, and promoting nonviolence and social justice. By embracing these principles and working together across religious and cultural divides, we can create a world where peace is not just a distant dream, but a lived reality.

ⁿⁿⁿ

Spiritual traditions offer a rich tapestry of insights into peace, emphasizing interconnectedness, compassion, and forgiveness. By finding common ground across diverse beliefs, we can tap into a wellspring of wisdom that can guide us towards a more peaceful and harmonious world. Let us embrace the spiritual dimensions of peace, for they offer a profound source of hope and inspiration.

TEN

PEACE AND JUSTICE: BUILDING A FAIR AND EQUITABLE WORLD

Peace and justice, two interconnected ideals, are fundamental to building a fair and equitable world. They are not mutually exclusive, but rather complementary and reinforcing concepts. While peace signifies the absence of conflict and violence, justice ensures that all individuals are treated with fairness, dignity, and respect. A world where peace prevails but justice is absent is not truly peaceful, as it is built on a foundation of inequality and resentment. Similarly, a world where justice is pursued through violent means undermines the very essence of peace. Therefore, it is essential to understand the intricate relationship between peace and justice and work towards their integration in creating a truly harmonious and equitable society.

The pursuit of justice is a fundamental human aspiration, rooted in our innate sense of fairness and morality. It is the cornerstone of any healthy and sustainable society. Justice encompasses a wide range of issues, including social, economic, and political equality, access to basic needs such as food, water, shelter, healthcare, and education, protection of human rights, and the rule of law. When these fundamental principles are upheld, it creates a sense of security and well-being, reducing the likelihood of conflict and violence.

However, the pursuit of justice can be complex and challenging, especially in societies marked by deep-rooted inequalities and historical injustices. It requires a multi-faceted approach that addresses the root causes of injustice, such as poverty, discrimination, and marginalization. This involves not only enacting laws and policies that promote equality and fairness but also changing attitudes and behaviors that perpetuate injustice.

Education plays a crucial role in promoting peace and justice. By teaching children about human rights, social justice, and conflict resolution, we can equip them with the knowledge and skills they need to become responsible and engaged citizens. Education can also help to break down stereotypes and prejudices, fostering understanding and respect for diversity.

Economic justice is another critical aspect of building a fair and equitable world. This involves ensuring that everyone has access to the resources and opportunities they need to live a decent life. It means tackling issues such as income inequality, poverty, and unemployment. When people have access to decent work and a fair share of resources, they are less likely to resort to violence and more likely to contribute to a peaceful and prosperous society.

Political justice is equally important. This involves ensuring that everyone has a voice in the decisions that affect their lives. It means promoting democracy, good governance, and the rule of law. When people feel that their voices are heard and that they have a stake in the political process, they are more likely to trust their institutions and to resolve conflicts peacefully.

Environmental justice is also an integral part of the peace and justice equation. Environmental degradation and climate change disproportionately affect the poor and marginalized, exacerbating existing inequalities and fueling conflict. Protecting the environment and ensuring that everyone has access to clean air, water, and land is essential for building a just and sustainable future.

The pursuit of peace and justice is not the responsibility of governments alone. It requires the active participation of civil society, businesses, and individuals. Civil society organizations can play a crucial role in advocating for justice, holding governments accountable, and providing services to marginalized communities. Businesses can contribute to peace and justice by adopting ethical practices, promoting fair trade, and supporting social and environmental initiatives. Individuals can make a difference by educating themselves about social issues, supporting organizations that work for peace and justice, and advocating for change in their communities.

The relationship between peace and justice is a dynamic and evolving one. It requires ongoing dialogue, negotiation, and compromise. There will inevitably be disagreements and conflicts along the way. However, by remaining committed to the principles of peace and justice, and by working together across differences, we can build a world that is more fair, equitable, and peaceful for all.

❦❦❦

Peace and justice are two sides of the same coin. A world without justice is not truly peaceful, and a world without peace cannot be just. Let us strive for a world where all individuals are treated with dignity, respect, and fairness, where the rule of law prevails, and where all voices are heard and valued.

ELEVEN

PEACE IN ACTION: INSPIRING STORIES OF CHANGEMAKERS

In the face of adversity and conflict, the human spirit has an uncanny ability to rise and inspire. Throughout history, there have been countless individuals who, through their unwavering commitment to peace, have become beacons of hope and catalysts for change. Their stories, often marked by courage, resilience, and compassion, serve as a testament to the power of individual action in creating a more peaceful and just world.

One such inspiring figure is Mahatma Gandhi, the leader of India's nonviolent independence movement. Gandhi's philosophy of nonviolence, or "ahimsa," emphasized the power of love, truth, and peaceful resistance in overcoming oppression. His unwavering commitment to nonviolence inspired millions around the world and ultimately led to India's independence from British rule. Gandhi's legacy continues to inspire peace activists and social movements globally, demonstrating the transformative power of nonviolent action.

Another remarkable changemaker is Nelson Mandela, the South African anti-apartheid revolutionary and politician who served as President of South Africa from 1994 to 1999. Mandela spent 27 years in prison for his activism against apartheid, a system of institutionalized racial segregation and discrimination. Despite the hardships he endured, Mandela emerged from prison with a message of reconciliation and forgiveness. He led South Africa through a peaceful transition to democracy, dismantling apartheid and establishing a new government based on equality and justice. Mandela's story is a testament to the power of forgiveness and reconciliation in healing a divided nation.

In the realm of environmental activism, Wangari Maathai stands out as a pioneer. Maathai, a Kenyan environmental and political activist, founded the Green Belt Movement, an environmental organization that empowers women to plant trees and conserve their environment. Through her tireless efforts, Maathai helped to restore degraded land, empower women, and raise awareness about the importance of environmental conservation. She was awarded the Nobel Peace Prize in 2004, recognizing her contributions to sustainable development, democracy, and peace.

Malala Yousafzai, a Pakistani activist for female education and the youngest Nobel Prize laureate, is another inspiring figure. At the age of 15, she was shot in the head by the Taliban for speaking out against their ban on girls' education. Despite the attack, Malala continued her advocacy, becoming a global symbol of the fight for girls' right to education. Her story is a testament to the power of courage and determination in overcoming adversity and fighting for what is right.

These are just a few examples of the many individuals who have dedicated their lives to peace. Their stories demonstrate that peace is not merely an abstract ideal, but a tangible reality that can be achieved through individual and collective action. They inspire us to believe in the power of our own actions, no matter how small, to make a positive difference in the world.

The changemakers of peace come from all walks of life, from different cultures, and with diverse backgrounds. What unites them is their unwavering commitment to peace, their courage in the face of adversity, and their compassion for others. Their stories remind us that peace is not a passive state, but an active pursuit that requires dedication, perseverance, and a willingness to take risks.

In today's world, where conflict and violence seem all too prevalent, the stories of these changemakers offer a glimmer of hope. They remind us that even in the darkest of times, the human spirit has the capacity to rise above adversity and create a better future. They inspire us to believe in the possibility of peace and to take action, no matter how small, to contribute to its realization.

ᐳᐳᐳ

The stories of changemakers inspire us to believe in the power of individual action to create a more peaceful world. Let us draw courage from their example, follow in their footsteps, and contribute our own unique threads to the tapestry of peace.

The Economics of Peace: Prosperity Through Cooperation

The economics of peace posits a fundamental truth: prosperity flourishes in an environment of cooperation and stability. The absence of conflict, both within and between nations, creates fertile ground for economic growth, innovation, and shared well-being. In contrast, war and violence impose significant economic costs, hindering development, disrupting trade, and perpetuating cycles of poverty. Recognizing the inextricable link between peace and prosperity is crucial for policymakers, businesses, and individuals alike to create a more stable, equitable, and thriving global economy.

At the national level, peace fosters an environment conducive to economic development. In times of peace, governments can allocate resources towards education, healthcare, infrastructure, and other essential services that improve the quality of life for their citizens. Businesses can invest with confidence, knowing that their operations are not threatened by conflict or instability. Individuals can pursue their livelihoods without fear of violence or displacement, leading to increased productivity and economic growth.

Trade, a cornerstone of the global economy, thrives in times of peace. Open borders and peaceful relations between nations facilitate the free flow of goods, services, and ideas. This, in turn, leads to increased competition, innovation, and specialization, driving economic growth and raising living standards. In contrast, war and conflict disrupt trade routes, impose sanctions, and create barriers to economic cooperation, hindering development and perpetuating poverty.

The economic costs of conflict are staggering. Wars consume vast amounts of resources that could otherwise be invested in education, healthcare, and infrastructure. They destroy infrastructure, disrupt livelihoods, and displace populations, leading to long-term economic hardship. The World Bank estimates that a single civil war can reduce a country's GDP by an average of 30 percent. Moreover, the economic consequences of conflict can extend far beyond the immediate zone of conflict, affecting global trade, investment, and financial markets.

In contrast, peace dividends are substantial. The resources saved from military spending can be redirected towards social and economic development, improving the lives of millions. Peace also fosters a climate of stability and predictability, attracting foreign investment and boosting economic growth. The experience of post-conflict countries like Rwanda and Mozambique demonstrates that peace can pave the way for rapid economic recovery and development.

The concept of peace through cooperation is not limited to the absence of conflict. It also involves actively working together to address shared challenges and achieve common goals. International cooperation on issues such as climate change, poverty, and disease can lead to solutions that benefit all nations. For example, the Paris Agreement on climate change demonstrates how countries can cooperate to address a global threat, while the Sustainable Development Goals provide a framework for international cooperation to eradicate poverty and promote prosperity.

Businesses also have a critical role to play in promoting peace and prosperity. By adopting ethical practices, supporting human rights, and investing in local communities, businesses can contribute to a more stable and equitable economic environment. Corporate social responsibility initiatives, such as fair trade and sustainable sourcing, can create economic opportunities for marginalized communities and contribute to peacebuilding efforts.

Individual actions also matter. By choosing to support businesses that prioritize peace and social responsibility, consumers can send a powerful message to the market. By investing in education and advocating for policies that promote peace and economic justice, individuals can help to create a more peaceful and prosperous world.

In conclusion, the economics of peace highlights the undeniable link between peace and prosperity. By investing in peace, we invest in our collective future. A peaceful world is not only a morally desirable outcome, but also an economically sound one. By fostering cooperation, promoting justice, and addressing the root causes of conflict, we can create a world where all individuals have the opportunity to thrive.

ppp

Peace is not just a moral imperative; it is also an economic necessity. Prosperity flourishes in an environment of cooperation and stability. By investing in peace, we invest in our collective well-being, creating a world where all can thrive.

THIRTEEN

PEACE AND THE ENVIRONMENT: PROTECTING OUR SHARED HOME

The interconnectedness of peace and the environment is undeniable. A healthy environment is essential for peaceful coexistence, while conflict and violence often lead to environmental degradation. Recognizing this interdependence is crucial for building a sustainable future where both humanity and nature can thrive.

Environmental degradation, such as deforestation, pollution, and climate change, poses significant threats to peace and security. Resource scarcity, exacerbated by environmental degradation, can lead to competition and conflict over dwindling resources like water, land, and food. This can destabilize communities, trigger displacement, and even ignite wars. For instance, the ongoing conflict in Darfur has been linked to desertification and water scarcity, highlighting the link between environmental stress and social unrest.

Climate change, a major consequence of environmental degradation, is a threat multiplier that exacerbates existing vulnerabilities and tensions. Rising sea levels, extreme weather events, and changes in precipitation patterns can lead to displacement, food insecurity, and economic disruption, all of which can fuel conflict and instability. The Syrian civil war, for instance, has been partially attributed to a prolonged drought that devastated the country's agricultural sector and displaced millions of people.

Conversely, a healthy environment is essential for peace. Access to clean water, fertile land, and a stable climate are fundamental for human well-being and social stability. Environmental protection can also foster cooperation and trust between communities and nations. For example, transboundary water management initiatives have proven to be effective in promoting peace and cooperation between countries that share water resources.

Recognizing the link between peace and the environment, the international community has increasingly focused on environmental peacebuilding. This approach aims to address the environmental factors that contribute to conflict and to promote environmental cooperation as a means of building peace. It involves a range of activities, such as restoring degraded ecosystems, promoting sustainable resource management, and supporting community-based initiatives that address environmental and social issues.

Environmental peacebuilding can take many forms. In post-conflict settings, it can involve restoring degraded ecosystems, promoting sustainable livelihoods, and facilitating dialogue between communities affected by environmental damage. In areas prone to conflict, environmental peacebuilding can focus on preventing conflict by addressing environmental stressors such as resource scarcity and climate change impacts.

International cooperation is also crucial for addressing global environmental challenges that threaten peace and security. The Paris Agreement on climate change, for example, is a landmark international accord that aims to limit global warming and mitigate its impacts. By working together to address this global threat, countries can not only protect the environment but also prevent future conflicts.

At the local level, community-based environmental initiatives can play a vital role in promoting peace. By involving local communities in environmental decision-making and resource management, these initiatives can empower people to take ownership of their environment and build resilience to environmental stressors. This, in turn, can reduce the risk of conflict and promote social cohesion.

The role of youth in environmental peacebuilding is also increasingly recognized. Young people are often at the forefront of environmental activism, advocating for change and demanding action from their leaders. By engaging youth in environmental decision-making and empowering them to become environmental stewards, we can create a generation of leaders committed to building a more peaceful and sustainable future.

The pursuit of peace and the protection of the environment are two sides of the same coin. A healthy environment is a prerequisite for peace, while peace is essential for environmental protection. By recognizing this interdependence and working together to address environmental challenges, we can create a world where both humanity and nature can thrive.

ᕤᕤᕤ

The environment is our shared home, and its health is inextricably linked to our own. Protecting our planet is not just an environmental issue, but a peace issue. By living in harmony with nature, we can ensure a sustainable and peaceful future for all.

FOURTEEN

WOMEN AND PEACE: THE POWER OF FEMININE LEADERSHIP

The role of women in peacebuilding is increasingly recognized as essential and transformative. Women bring unique perspectives, skills, and experiences to the table, challenging traditional power dynamics and advocating for inclusive and sustainable solutions. Their leadership, often characterized by empathy, collaboration, and a focus on community well-being, has proven to be instrumental in preventing conflict, resolving disputes, and building lasting peace.

Historically, women have been marginalized in formal peace processes and decision-making bodies. However, their contributions to peace at the grassroots level have always been significant. Women often play a crucial role in their communities as caregivers, educators, and peacemakers. They are often the first to respond to conflict, providing support and resources to those affected by violence. Their deep understanding of their communities and their ability to build trust and relationships make them invaluable assets in peacebuilding efforts.

Research has shown that women's participation in peace processes leads to more sustainable and lasting peace agreements. A study by the Council on Foreign Relations found that peace agreements are 35% more likely to last at least 15 years when women are involved in their negotiation. This is because women tend to prioritize issues such as social justice, human rights, and economic development, which are essential for building a lasting peace.

Women's leadership in peacebuilding is also characterized by a focus on inclusivity and collaboration. They often work across traditional divides, bringing together diverse stakeholders to find common ground and build consensus. This approach is essential for addressing the root causes of conflict and creating sustainable solutions that benefit all members of society.

Furthermore, women's leadership often emphasizes the importance of dialogue and nonviolence. They are more likely to advocate for peaceful solutions and to prioritize the needs of vulnerable groups, such as women, children, and the elderly. Their approach to conflict resolution often involves building relationships, fostering trust, and promoting understanding between different groups.

The power of feminine leadership is evident in many peacebuilding initiatives around the world. In Liberia, women played a pivotal role in ending the country's brutal civil war. Leymah Gbowee, a Liberian peace activist, organized a mass movement of women that used nonviolent tactics such as strikes and protests to demand an end to the violence. Their efforts ultimately led to peace talks and the election of Ellen Johnson Sirleaf, Africa's first elected female head of state.

In Northern Ireland, women from both sides of the conflict came together to form the Northern Ireland Women's Coalition, a political party that advocated for peace and reconciliation. Their participation in the peace process was instrumental in bringing about the Good Friday Agreement, which ended decades of violence.

In Colombia, women played a crucial role in the peace talks that ended the country's 52-year civil war with the FARC guerrilla group. They were instrumental in ensuring that the peace agreement included provisions for gender equality and women's participation in the post-conflict reconstruction process.

These are just a few examples of the many ways in which women are contributing to peacebuilding efforts around the world. Their leadership, characterized by empathy, collaboration, and a focus on community well-being, is essential for building a more peaceful and just world.

However, despite the significant contributions of women to peace, they continue to face numerous challenges. They are often excluded from formal peace processes, denied access to resources, and subjected to violence and discrimination. Overcoming these obstacles requires a concerted effort to promote gender equality, empower women, and ensure their full participation in decision-making processes at all levels.

The world needs more women leaders in peacebuilding. Their unique perspectives, skills, and experiences are essential for creating sustainable solutions to complex challenges. By investing in women's leadership, we can build a more peaceful, just, and equitable world for all.

ppp

Women's leadership, often characterized by empathy, collaboration, and a focus on community, is essential for building lasting peace. Let us empower women and girls to become leaders in their communities, for their voices and perspectives are invaluable in creating a more just and equitable world.

FIFTEEN

INDIGENOUS WISDOM: ANCIENT TRADITIONS FOR PEACE

Indigenous cultures worldwide, rich in history and wisdom, offer unique and invaluable perspectives on peace. These ancient traditions, deeply rooted in a profound understanding of nature, community, and spirituality, provide a blueprint for harmonious living that resonates across generations. By exploring indigenous wisdom, we can gain valuable insights into fostering peace within ourselves, our communities, and our relationship with the natural world.

At the heart of many indigenous traditions is a deep respect for nature. Indigenous peoples view themselves as part of a larger interconnected web of life, recognizing the interdependence of all living beings. They believe that harmony with nature is essential for both individual and collective well-being. This respect is often reflected in their practices of sustainable resource management, reverence for sacred sites, and rituals that celebrate the cycles of nature.

Indigenous cultures also place a strong emphasis on community and interconnectedness. They value cooperation, sharing, and mutual support as essential for survival and well-being. Decision-making processes often involve extensive consultation and consensus-building, ensuring that all voices are heard and that decisions are made in the best interest of the community as a whole.

This emphasis on community fosters a sense of belonging and shared responsibility, creating a foundation for peaceful coexistence.

Spirituality is often interwoven with indigenous concepts of peace. Many indigenous cultures believe in a spiritual connection to the land, ancestors, and the natural world. This connection is often expressed through rituals, ceremonies, and storytelling, which serve to transmit cultural values and knowledge from one generation to the next.

These spiritual practices can foster a sense of inner peace, connection to community, and reverence for the natural world.

Conflict resolution within indigenous communities often involves restorative justice practices that prioritize healing and reconciliation. These practices focus on addressing the harm caused by the conflict, repairing relationships, and restoring harmony within the community.

Elders and other respected members of the community often play a crucial role in facilitating these processes, drawing on their wisdom and experience to guide the parties towards a peaceful resolution.

Indigenous wisdom also offers valuable insights into the prevention of conflict. Many indigenous cultures emphasize the importance of early intervention and addressing the root causes of conflict, such as poverty, inequality, and social injustice. They also prioritize communication, dialogue, and understanding as key tools for preventing conflict from escalating.

The concept of peace in many indigenous cultures is holistic, encompassing not only the absence of violence but also a state of physical, emotional, mental, and spiritual well-being. This holistic approach recognizes that peace is not just about the absence of conflict but also about creating conditions that allow individuals and communities to thrive.

Indigenous knowledge and practices have much to offer the world in its pursuit of peace. Their emphasis on interconnectedness, community, respect for nature, and restorative justice offers valuable lessons for building a more peaceful and sustainable future.

By recognizing and valuing indigenous wisdom, we can learn from their ancient traditions and apply them to our modern challenges.

However, indigenous peoples have often been marginalized and their knowledge and practices dismissed as outdated or irrelevant. This has led to the loss of valuable knowledge and cultural practices, as well as the displacement and marginalization of indigenous communities.

It is essential to recognize the contributions of indigenous peoples to peacebuilding and to support their efforts to preserve their cultures and traditions.

In recent years, there has been a growing recognition of the importance of indigenous knowledge and practices in addressing global challenges such as climate change, conflict, and social inequality.

Indigenous peoples are increasingly being invited to participate in international forums and decision-making processes, sharing their wisdom and perspectives with the world.

By learning from indigenous wisdom and incorporating their practices into our own lives, we can create a more peaceful, just, and sustainable world for all.

ϼϼϼ

Indigenous wisdom, rooted in a deep connection to nature and community, offers valuable lessons for peaceful living. Let us learn from their traditions, respect their knowledge, and work together to build a world that honors the interconnectedness of all life.

SIXTEEN

Peace through Technology: Connecting a Global Community

In an increasingly interconnected world, technology has emerged as a double-edged sword in the pursuit of peace. On one hand, it has the potential to bridge divides, foster understanding, and amplify voices for peace. On the other hand, it can be misused to spread misinformation, incite violence, and exacerbate conflict. However, when harnessed for good, technology can play a pivotal role in building a global community rooted in peace, understanding, and cooperation.

One of the most significant ways technology contributes to peace is by facilitating communication and connection across borders. The internet, social media platforms, and video conferencing tools have broken down geographical barriers, enabling individuals from different cultures and backgrounds to interact and learn from each other. This exchange of ideas and perspectives can foster empathy, reduce prejudice, and build bridges of understanding between diverse communities.

Furthermore, technology has empowered marginalized groups and given them a platform to voice their concerns and advocate for their rights. Social media platforms, for example, have been instrumental in amplifying the voices of activists, protesters, and human rights defenders, allowing them to mobilize support and raise awareness of issues that might otherwise go unnoticed. This increased visibility can pressure governments and institutions to address grievances and uphold human rights, contributing to a more just and peaceful society.

Technology has also facilitated the emergence of citizen journalism and independent media, providing alternative narratives to those often presented by mainstream media. This diversification of information sources can help to counter propaganda and misinformation, promoting a more balanced and nuanced understanding of complex issues. By empowering individuals to access and share information, technology can promote transparency and accountability, crucial elements for building trust and preventing conflict.

In the realm of conflict resolution and peacebuilding, technology has opened up new avenues for dialogue and mediation. Online platforms can facilitate virtual meetings and negotiations, allowing parties in conflict to engage in constructive dialogue without the need for physical proximity. This can be particularly valuable in situations where travel is restricted or where face-to-face meetings are not feasible.

Technology has also enabled the development of innovative tools for monitoring and preventing conflict. Satellite imagery, for instance, can be used to track troop movements, identify potential flashpoints, and monitor human rights violations. Early warning systems that utilize data analysis and predictive modeling can help to identify emerging conflicts and provide early intervention to prevent them from escalating.

Crowdsourcing platforms have proven to be effective tools for conflict monitoring and peacebuilding. By harnessing the power of citizen reporting, these platforms can provide real-time information about events on the ground, helping to verify information and counter misinformation. They can also be used to mobilize support for humanitarian aid and peacebuilding initiatives.

Artificial intelligence (AI) and machine learning are also being utilized in the pursuit of peace. AI-powered tools can analyze vast amounts of data to identify patterns and trends that can help to predict and prevent conflict. They can also be used to translate languages, facilitate communication across cultural divides, and personalize peacebuilding messages to different audiences.

However, the use of technology for peace is not without its challenges. The same tools that can be used to promote peace can also be weaponized to spread hate speech, incite violence, and manipulate public opinion. The rise of cyber warfare, disinformation campaigns, and online radicalization pose serious threats to peace and security.

To harness the full potential of technology for peace, it is crucial to address these challenges and ensure that technology is used ethically and responsibly. This involves promoting digital literacy, critical thinking, and media literacy to empower individuals to discern fact from fiction and to resist manipulation. It also requires robust cybersecurity measures to protect against cyberattacks and the spread of harmful content.

Collaboration between governments, civil society organizations, tech companies, and individuals is essential for maximizing the positive impact of technology on peace. By working together to develop ethical guidelines, invest in peace tech initiatives, and promote digital inclusion, we can harness the power of technology to build a more peaceful and connected global community.

❦❦❦

Technology, when used for good, can be a powerful tool for peace. It can connect us across borders, amplify voices for justice, and facilitate dialogue and understanding. Let us harness the power of technology to build bridges of peace, not walls of division.

SEVENTEEN

Peace in Everyday Life: Simple Practices for Harmony

In our fast-paced and often chaotic world, finding peace in everyday life can seem like an elusive goal. However, peace is not a distant destination or a grand event, but a state of mind that can be cultivated through simple practices and conscious choices. It is not about eliminating all challenges or difficulties, but rather about finding a sense of inner calm and resilience in the midst of life's ups and downs. By integrating these practices into our daily routines, we can transform our lives and contribute to a more peaceful and harmonious world.

One of the most fundamental practices for cultivating peace is mindfulness. This involves paying attention to the present moment without judgment, observing our thoughts and emotions without getting caught up in them. Mindfulness can be practiced through formal meditation or simply by bringing awareness to everyday activities, such as eating, walking, or washing dishes. By anchoring ourselves in the present moment, we can reduce stress and anxiety, increase self-awareness, and develop a greater sense of inner peace.

Another simple yet powerful practice is gratitude. Taking the time to appreciate the good things in our lives, no matter how small, can shift our focus from what we lack to what we have, fostering a sense of contentment and well-being. Gratitude can be practiced through journaling, expressing appreciation to others, or simply taking a moment each day to reflect on the things we are grateful for.

Acts of kindness, both big and small, can also contribute to peace in everyday life. Helping a neighbor, volunteering in the community, or simply offering a smile or a kind word to a stranger can create a ripple effect of positivity and goodwill. By focusing on helping others, we shift our attention away from our own problems and concerns, fostering a sense of connection and purpose.

Forgiveness is another essential practice for cultivating peace. Holding onto anger and resentment towards others only harms ourselves, preventing us from moving forward and finding peace. Forgiveness does not mean condoning hurtful behavior, but rather choosing to release negative emotions and open our hearts to compassion and understanding.

Taking care of our physical and mental health is also crucial for inner peace. Regular exercise, healthy eating, and adequate sleep can all contribute to a sense of well-being. Engaging in activities that we enjoy, such as spending time in nature, listening to music, or pursuing creative hobbies, can also nourish our souls and bring us joy.

Maintaining healthy relationships is another important aspect of peace in everyday life. This involves communicating openly and honestly with loved ones, resolving conflicts constructively, and practicing empathy and compassion. Building strong social connections can provide us with support, comfort, and a sense of belonging, all of which contribute to inner peace.

Cultivating a positive mindset is also essential. This involves challenging negative thoughts and beliefs, focusing on solutions rather than problems, and practicing self-compassion. By reframing our thoughts and focusing on the positive, we can create a more optimistic and hopeful outlook on life.

In addition to these individual practices, there are also collective actions we can take to promote peace in our communities and the world. This includes advocating for social justice, supporting peacebuilding initiatives, and engaging in dialogue with people from different backgrounds. By working together to address the root causes of conflict and violence, we can create a more peaceful and just world for all.

Peace is not a destination, but a journey. It requires ongoing effort and commitment. However, by incorporating simple practices into our daily lives, we can cultivate inner peace, build stronger relationships, and contribute to a more harmonious world. The journey towards peace begins with each of us, one step at a time.

Peace is not a distant ideal, but a daily practice. Through mindfulness, gratitude, forgiveness, and kindness, we can weave peace into the fabric of our everyday lives, creating a ripple effect that extends outwards to our families, communities, and the world.

EIGHTEEN

THE FUTURE OF PEACE: EMERGING TRENDS AND CHALLENGES

The future of peace is a complex tapestry woven with threads of hope, innovation, and resilience, yet it also faces significant challenges that threaten to unravel the progress made towards a more harmonious world. Emerging trends in technology, social movements, and global cooperation offer promising avenues for peacebuilding, but they are juxtaposed with persistent threats such as climate change, inequality, and political polarization. Navigating these complex and interconnected challenges requires a nuanced understanding of the evolving landscape of peace and a commitment to finding innovative and sustainable solutions.

One of the most promising trends in the future of peace is the increasing role of technology in conflict prevention and resolution. Artificial intelligence, big data analytics, and social media platforms are being leveraged to monitor conflict hotspots, predict outbreaks of violence, and promote dialogue and understanding between different groups. For instance, AI-powered tools can analyze vast amounts of data from social media and news sources to identify patterns and trends that may indicate rising tensions or potential conflict triggers. This early warning system can enable policymakers and peacebuilders to intervene proactively, preventing conflicts from escalating into violence.

Social media platforms, while often criticized for their role in spreading misinformation and hate speech, also have the potential to be powerful tools for peacebuilding. They can connect individuals from different backgrounds, foster cross-cultural understanding, and amplify the voices of peace activists and marginalized communities. Grassroots movements for peace and social justice have harnessed the power of social media to mobilize support, raise awareness, and advocate for change.

Another promising trend is the growing recognition of the importance of inclusivity and diversity in peacebuilding. Women, youth, and marginalized groups are increasingly being recognized as essential stakeholders in peace processes. Their perspectives and experiences are invaluable in addressing the root causes of conflict and building sustainable peace. The inclusion of these diverse voices can lead to more holistic and effective solutions that address the needs of all members of society.

Global cooperation and multilateralism are also crucial for addressing transnational challenges that threaten peace and security. Climate change, pandemics, and economic inequality are global problems that require global solutions. International organizations, such as the United Nations, play a vital role in facilitating dialogue, coordinating efforts, and providing resources for peacebuilding initiatives.

However, the future of peace also faces significant challenges. Climate change, one of the most pressing issues of our time, poses a major threat to peace and security. As resources become scarcer and extreme weather events become more frequent, the risk of conflict over land, water, and food will increase. Climate-induced displacement and migration can also exacerbate social tensions and create new sources of conflict.

Economic inequality, both within and between countries, is another major challenge to peace. Poverty, unemployment, and lack of opportunities can fuel resentment and frustration, leading to social unrest and violence. Addressing economic inequality through equitable distribution of resources, job creation, and investment in education and healthcare is crucial for building a more peaceful and just society.

Political polarization and the rise of extremist ideologies also pose significant threats to peace. The spread of hate speech, misinformation, and propaganda through social media and other online platforms can fuel division, mistrust, and violence. Addressing these challenges requires promoting media literacy, critical thinking, and dialogue, as well as strengthening democratic institutions and the rule of law.

In conclusion, the future of peace is a complex and dynamic landscape shaped by both promising trends and daunting challenges. The increasing role of technology, the rise of social movements, and the growing emphasis on inclusivity and global cooperation offer hope for a more peaceful world. However, the persistent threats of climate change, economic inequality, and political polarization require urgent and concerted action. By embracing innovation, fostering dialogue, and promoting justice and equity, we can navigate these challenges and build a future where peace is not just an aspiration but a reality.

ppp

The future of peace is in our hands. As we face unprecedented challenges, let us embrace innovation, foster dialogue, and promote justice and equity. By working together, we can navigate the complexities of our world and build a future where peace is not just an aspiration, but a lived reality.

NINETEEN

A Tapestry of Hope: Celebrating Global Efforts for Peace

Amidst the seemingly endless cycle of conflict and violence that plagues our world, a tapestry of hope is being woven, thread by thread, by individuals and organizations across the globe dedicated to the pursuit of peace. These global efforts, diverse in their approaches and contexts, collectively represent a beacon of hope, illuminating a path towards a more harmonious and equitable world. By celebrating these initiatives and recognizing their impact, we can inspire further action and strengthen the collective resolve to build a lasting peace.

From grassroots movements to international organizations, countless actors are working tirelessly to prevent conflict, resolve disputes, and promote reconciliation. These efforts span a wide range of activities, from mediation and dialogue to disarmament and peace education. They involve individuals from all walks of life, including activists, religious leaders, educators, policymakers, and ordinary citizens who are committed to making a difference.

One of the most inspiring examples of global peace efforts is the work of non-governmental organizations (NGOs) that operate in conflict zones around the world. These organizations provide humanitarian aid, support peace negotiations, and implement programs aimed at reconciliation and rebuilding communities torn apart by war. Their work often involves enormous risks and challenges, yet they persevere in their commitment to peace, driven by the belief that even in the darkest of times, hope can prevail.

Another important aspect of global peace efforts is the work of international organizations such as the United Nations. The UN plays a crucial role in promoting peace and security through its various agencies and programs. It facilitates dialogue between conflicting parties, deploys peacekeepers to conflict zones, and provides humanitarian assistance to those affected by war. The UN also works to address the root causes of conflict, such as poverty, inequality, and injustice, through its development and human rights programs.

The role of religious and spiritual leaders in peacebuilding is also significant. Many religious traditions emphasize the importance of peace, compassion, and forgiveness. Religious leaders can use their influence to promote dialogue, reconciliation, and nonviolence. They can also provide spiritual support and guidance to those affected by conflict, helping them to heal and rebuild their lives.

Education plays a crucial role in fostering a culture of peace. Peace education programs teach children and young people about conflict resolution, human rights, and intercultural understanding. They empower individuals to become active participants in building a more peaceful and just society. By investing in peace education, we are investing in the future of our world.

The arts also have a powerful role to play in peacebuilding. Music, theater, dance, and visual arts can transcend cultural boundaries and connect people on a deeper level. They can express the pain and suffering caused by conflict, as well as the resilience and hope that emerge from it. Art can also be a tool for dialogue and reconciliation, bringing together people from different backgrounds to share their stories and perspectives.

The media, too, can contribute to peacebuilding efforts. By reporting on conflict in a responsible and balanced way, the media can raise awareness of the human cost of war and the importance of finding peaceful solutions. They can also highlight positive stories of peace and reconciliation, inspiring others to take action.

The global movement for peace is not without its challenges. Conflicts continue to rage in many parts of the world, fueled by factors such as political instability, economic inequality, and religious extremism. The rise of nationalism and populism in some countries also poses a threat to international cooperation and peacebuilding efforts.

However, despite these challenges, there is reason for hope. The global tapestry of peace is woven with countless threads of courage, compassion, and determination. By celebrating these efforts and recognizing their impact, we can strengthen the collective resolve to build a more peaceful and just world for all.

ൟൟൟ

The tapestry of peace is woven with countless threads of hope, resilience, and determination. Let us celebrate the global efforts for peace, recognizing the progress made and the challenges ahead. Together, we can create a world where all beings can thrive in harmony.

TWENTY

WEAVING OUR OWN THREADS: A PERSONAL JOURNEY TO PEACE

The journey towards peace is not merely a global pursuit, but an intimate, personal odyssey that each individual embarks upon. It's a continuous process of self-discovery, introspection, and transformation. Weaving our own threads of peace involves navigating the complexities of our inner world, healing past wounds, and cultivating a mindset of compassion, understanding, and acceptance. It's about finding harmony within ourselves, which then radiates outwards, creating a ripple effect of peace in our relationships, communities, and the world at large.

The first step in this journey is self-awareness. It requires us to delve deep within ourselves, to understand our thoughts, emotions, and behaviors. This involves acknowledging our strengths and weaknesses, recognizing our triggers, and understanding the underlying causes of our actions. Self-awareness is not about judgment or criticism, but about acceptance and understanding. It allows us to see ourselves with clarity and compassion, paving the way for personal growth and transformation.

The second step is healing. We all carry within us the scars of past hurts and traumas. These wounds, if left unaddressed, can fester and create internal conflict, hindering our ability to find peace. Healing involves acknowledging and processing these emotions, allowing ourselves to feel the pain, and gradually letting go of the past. This can be facilitated through various means, such as therapy, journaling, or simply spending time in quiet reflection. Healing is not about erasing the past, but about transforming its impact on our present and future.

Cultivating positive emotions is the next step in our journey. Emotions like gratitude, compassion, joy, and love have a profound impact on our well-being. Gratitude helps us to appreciate the good things in our lives, while compassion allows us to connect with the suffering of others and extend a helping hand. Joy and love fill our hearts with warmth and positivity, making us more resilient in the face of adversity. By consciously cultivating these emotions, we can create a more peaceful and joyful inner landscape.

Mindfulness, the practice of being fully present in the moment, is another crucial aspect of weaving our own threads of peace. It involves paying attention to our thoughts, emotions, and bodily sensations without judgment. By anchoring ourselves in the present moment, we can break free from the cycle of rumination and worry, reducing stress and anxiety. Mindfulness also allows us to cultivate a deeper connection with ourselves and the world around us, fostering a sense of peace and well-being.

Building healthy relationships is also essential in our journey towards peace. Our relationships with others have a profound impact on our emotional and mental well-being. By nurturing positive relationships, communicating openly and honestly, and resolving conflicts constructively, we can create a supportive and loving environment that fosters peace.

Contributing to our communities and the world at large is another way to weave our own threads of peace. By volunteering our time, donating to causes we care about, or simply being kind and compassionate towards others, we can create a positive impact on the world around us. This sense of purpose and contribution can bring immense fulfillment and peace.

The journey to peace is not a linear path, but a continuous process of growth and evolution. There will be setbacks and challenges along the way. However, by embracing self-awareness, healing, positive emotions, mindfulness, healthy relationships, and community engagement, we can navigate these challenges and weave a tapestry of peace that enriches our lives and the lives of those around us.

Remember, peace is not a destination, but a journey. It starts within each of us, with the conscious choice to cultivate peace in our own hearts and minds. By weaving our own threads of peace, we contribute to a collective tapestry of hope and harmony, creating a more peaceful and just world for all.

ᐅᐅᐅ

The journey towards peace begins within each of us. By cultivating inner peace, fostering compassion, and embracing our interconnectedness, we can become agents of change, weaving our own unique threads into the tapestry of peace.

TWENTY-ONE
SUMMARY

In exploring the tapestry of peace, we have embarked on a journey that traverses cultures, philosophies, and practices. We've delved into the ancient wisdom of diverse civilizations, seeking timeless teachings on harmony that resonate across centuries. We've examined the profound power of language, both in inciting conflict and fostering peace, and explored how communication and conflict resolution can bridge divides and build understanding. We've sought solace and tranquility in nature's symphony, recognizing the profound connection between a healthy environment and peaceful coexistence.

Our journey has led us inwards, to cultivate inner peace through mindfulness, gratitude, and compassion. We've recognized the transformative power of forgiveness as a path to reconciliation and healing, both within ourselves and in our relationships with others. We've celebrated the inspiring stories of changemakers who have dedicated their lives to peace, demonstrating the impact that individual and collective action can have on creating a more just and harmonious world.

We've delved into the economics of peace, recognizing that prosperity flourishes in an environment of cooperation and stability. We've explored the intricate relationship between peace and justice, acknowledging that a truly peaceful world must also be a fair and equitable one. We've examined the vital role of women in peacebuilding, their unique leadership styles, and the power of feminine perspectives in creating lasting peace.

We've learned from indigenous wisdom, drawing on ancient traditions that emphasize interconnectedness, community, and respect for nature. We've explored the potential of technology to connect a global community, facilitating dialogue, amplifying voices for peace, and promoting understanding across cultures. We've discovered simple practices for incorporating peace into our everyday lives, through mindfulness, gratitude, forgiveness, and acts of kindness.

Looking towards the future, we've acknowledged the emerging trends and challenges that will shape the path towards peace. Technological advancements, social movements, and global cooperation offer promising avenues for peacebuilding, but they are juxtaposed with persistent threats such as climate change, inequality, and political polarization. Navigating these complex challenges requires a multi-faceted approach that addresses the root causes of conflict, promotes inclusivity and diversity, and fosters a culture of peace.

Ultimately, the pursuit of peace is a collective endeavor that requires the active participation of individuals, communities, and nations. It's about weaving our own threads of peace, cultivating inner harmony, and working together to create a world where all beings can thrive. It's about celebrating the global efforts for peace, recognizing the progress made, and remaining committed to the journey ahead.

As we move forward, let us draw inspiration from the countless individuals and organizations who have dedicated themselves to the cause of peace. Let us learn from their wisdom, emulate their courage, and continue their legacy. The path to peace may be long and arduous, but the rewards are immeasurable. A peaceful world is not just a dream, but a possibility that we can create together, one step at a time.

ᎧᎧᎧ

Citation And References

This book represents the culmination of extensive research and meticulous analysis, incorporating a diverse range of sources, including numerous books, scholarly studies, and personal experiences. Additionally, I have scoured various websites to gather relevant information and data essential for the compilation of this work. I have taken every precaution to ensure the accuracy of the information presented and have diligently cited all sources to acknowledge their contributions.

Despite these efforts, the possibility of inadvertent errors remains. I deeply value the insights of my readers and appreciate any feedback that can help identify and rectify such inaccuracies. I encourage you to bring any discrepancies to my attention.

Your feedback is not only welcome but crucial, as it will aid in correcting current editions and enhancing the content of future ones. I am committed to maintaining the highest standards of accuracy and reliability in my work and thank you for your support and understanding.

Additionally, I firmly uphold the principle of freedom of speech and expression as guaranteed under Article 19(1)(a) of the Constitution of India, and I respect the diverse viewpoints and expressions of all readers.

ϼϼϼ

Other Books Of The Author

1. Empowering Minds: A Journey into Women's Self-Discovery and Power
2. The Dynamics of Motivation: Catalyzing Thought into Action
3. Meditation and Mental Well Being: The Path to Inner Peace and Clarity
4. The Psychology of Child Education: Nurturing Future Generations
5. Ethical Enlightenment: A Modern Guide to Living with Integrity
6. Voices of Empowerment: Stories of Women Rising Against Odds
7. Social Psychology in Everyday Life: Understanding Human Connections
8. The Essence of Motivational Speaking: Inspiring Change in Others
9. Balancing Acts: Women, Work, and the Will to Lead
10. Guiding with Grace: Raising Children with Compassion and Awareness
11. The Power of Positive Aging: Embracing Life After Fifty
12. Building Resilient Communities: Social Work in Action
13. The Ethical Educator: Principles for Teaching and Learning
14. From Insight to Impact: Social Psychology for a Better World
15. The Ethics of Empathy: A Guide to Ethical Living
16. The Science of Empowering the Self: Navigating Life's Challenges with Psychological Wisdom
17. The Mindful Conscious Leader: Meditation Techniques for Modern Management
18. Pioneering Spirit: Women's Pathways to Leadership and Empowerment
19. Feeling to Healing: The Role of Emotional Intelligence in Child Development
20. Transformative Talks and Words of Inspiration: Insights into Motivational Oratory

in a Complex World

46. Secret of Solopreneur's Odyssey: Navigating the Path to Self-Employment

47. Exploring Tapestry of Peace: Global Perspectives on Harmony

48. The Art and Actions of Connection: Mastering Communication for Impact

49. She Governs and at the Helm: Strategies for Political Empowerment

50. Rising Above and Rising with Grace: A Woman's Roadmap to Career Mastery

51. The Effect of Networking & Connectedness: Building Strategic Alliances for Women

52. Beyond his Barriers: Women Thriving in Male-Dominated Fields

53. Secret of Inner Compass: Navigating Life with Intuition

54. Creative & Pro-Active Muses: A Celebration of Women in the Arts

55. Unburdened: The Art of Releasing the Past

56. Amplified Voices: Speeches of Women that Astonished the World

57. Secret of Manifesting Dreams: A Woman's Guide to Intentional Living

58. Ethics and Value Based Education: Reimagining Japan's School System

59. The Moral Compass Curriculum: A Holistic Approach

60. Tech with Heart: Integrating Ethics into Digital Learning

61. Honoring Virtue: Recognizing Ethical Excellence in Education

62. Raising Good Humans: A Guide to Character Development

63. The Spark Within: Nurturing Creativity in Children

64. The Teenager Whisperer: Navigating Adolescence with Grace

65. Igniting a Passion for Learning: Inspiring Lifelong Curiosity

66. The Habit Lab: Cultivating Positive Behaviors in Children

67. Seeds of Empathy: Fostering Compassion in Young Hearts

68. The Reading Revolution: Inspiring a Love of Books in Children

69. The Learning Brain: Unlocking the Secrets of Student Success

70. Teaching for All: Differentiated Instruction Strategies

71. The Time Alchemist: Mastering Time Management for Peak Performance

Bhajan
101. Pilgrimage of the Soul: Spiritual Journeys in India

ϘϘϘ

• 131 •

Contact

Dr. Minakshi Bansal
Social Activist
Ahmedabad, Gujarat, Bharat
minakshiindiag20@yahoo.com

❦❦❦

|| LOKAHA SAMASTHAHA SUKHINO BHAVANTU ||